The Robert McCloskey Connection

by Will C. Howell

FEARON TEACHER AIDS
Simon & Schuster Supplementary Education Group

Robert McCloskey,

*Thank-you for becoming an inventor of words, pictures, and books.
You have been a musician too—orchestrating life with brush and pen
and leaving your strains of joy and wonder in the hearts of your
readers. Thank-you for letting me have the opportunity to do this
book. I hope it will bring learning, life, and literature closer together
for children and adults.*

Will Howell

Editor: Carol Williams
Copyeditor: Cynthia Seagren
Illustration: Gwen Connelly
Cover illustration: Sally Cox
Design: Diann Abbott

ISBN 0-8224-5829-2

Printed in the United States of America
1. 9 8 7 6 5 4 3 2 1

Contents

Introduction

The emphasis on "The Year of the Young Reader" (1989) and "International Literacy Year" (1990) has helped children's literature come of age. Research confirms that good reading and writing are best taught by using good books. And today, educators are fortunate to have a wide selection of excellent children's books to choose from.

The Robert McCloskey Connection is written for librarians and teachers who want to effectively use good literature in their classrooms. The lessons present art, math, creative writing, science, and social studies activities to accompany books by this one outstanding author. The variety of interdisciplinary activities and the whole-language instructional approach incorporated in the lessons will help you meet the diverse needs and interests of your students.

As students become familiar with various works by a single author, they develop an ability to analyze literary and artistic style. Children can go to the library and select books written or illustrated by authors they feel as if they have actually met. "Connecting" with authors stimulates students to become more involved in and enthusiastic about reading, writing, and learning. *The Robert McCloskey Connection* gives students the opportunity to meet an author/illustrator who has remained popular for over fifty years.

Lessons require minimal preparation, while resulting in maximum participation and learning. A brief synopsis of each book is included at the beginning of the section containing activities complementing that particular book. Read the book aloud to the children and invite them to enjoy the illustrations before participating in the activities. Activities ranging from writing clam stories to painting with blueberries will allow you to enhance and reinforce your curriculum.

Meet Robert McCloskey

Robert McCloskey was born on September 15, 1914, in Hamilton, Ohio.

As a young boy, Robert played the piano, oboe, and harmonica and dreamed of one day becoming a musician. But he, like many other young children, soon changed his mind about his future plans. He decided to become an inventor, and this dream became a reality. Robert McCloskey used his inventiveness to write and illustrate many books that are still enjoyed today, many years after their creation.

Not only did Robert McCloskey's desire to be an inventor manifest itself in the publication of many excellent children's books, but he also included his inventiveness in the content of his books. In 1940, Robert McCloskey wrote his first book, *Lentil*, about a young boy with adventures and dreams much like his own. Later, Robert's fascination with invention showed up in *Homer Price*. After observing the predicament of ducklings in Boston traffic, Robert McCloskey began one of his most well-known inventive experiments. Mr. McCloskey took some ducklings home to his apartment and began to draw them. The experiment was a success. Today, 45 years later, *Make Way for Ducklings* is still a favorite with children and adults. Robert McCloskey also won the Caldecott Award in 1942 for his ingenious illustrations in that book.

Mr. McCloskey enjoys gardening and sailing in Maine, the setting for *Blueberries for Sal, One Morning in Maine, Burt Dow, Deep-Water Man,* and his second Caldecott Award book (1958) *Time of Wonder.*

Blueberries

On a summer day in Maine, a little girl and a bear cub wandered away from their blueberry-picking mothers and stumbled upon each other. This is the kind of bear-went-over-the-mountain story that young children like to tell and retell.

New York: Viking Press, 1948

for Sal

❧ • PAINTING • ❧

Materials:

- •blueberries
- •plastic spoons
- •paintbrushes
- •paper cups
- •drawing paper

Lesson Procedure

1. Give each student a paper cup with one tablespoon of blueberries.
2. Pass out the remaining materials and have students crush the berries with their spoons. (It is not necessary to add water.)
3. Using their paintbrushes, students can paint pictures with the blueberry juice. The "paint" will actually be magenta in color.
4. Have primary childen wear paint shirts to protect their clothing.

Taking It Further . . .

Discuss other natural materials that could be used for making paint (other types of berries, fruit, vegetables, flowers). Encourage students to bring these materials for the next art lesson. Send home a letter of explanation to parents.

Materials:

•lined paper
•pencils

Lesson Procedure

1. Have the children recall the search efforts made by Sal, Little Bear, and both mothers. List them on the board.

   Sal heard a noise—looked around a rock—found crows
   Sal heard a noise—looked in the bushes—found Little Bear's mother
   Little Bear heard a noise—looked over a stump—found a partridge and family
   Little Bear heard a noise—looked in the bushes—found Sal's mother
   Sal's mother heard kuplink! kuplank! kuplunk!—found Sal
   Little Bear's mother heard rustling and munching sounds—found Little Bear

2. Compare and discuss the similarities in all four characters' behavior.
3. Let children share experiences they have had searching for their mothers or fathers after wandering off in a store or park.
4. Have children construct well-written paragraphs or creative stories based on their experiences.

Taking It Further . . .

Children can draw maps of Sal's and Little Bear's searches.

SEQUENCING

Materials:

- worksheet on page 11
- drawing paper
- scissors
- glue

Lesson Procedure

1. Pass out the worksheet to each student and read it together.
2. Begin discussing which sentence on the worksheet happened first in the story, second, third, and so on.
3. Instruct the students to cut the sentences apart and arrange them in the order in which they happened.
4. Have the students glue the cutout sentences in order on drawing paper.

Worksheet Answer Key

1. Sal and her mother went to pick blueberries.
2. Sal sat down in a large clump of bushes and ate blueberries.
3. Little Bear sat down in a large clump of bushes and ate blueberries.
4. Little Sal heard a noise and found some crows.
5. Little Sal heard a noise and found Little Bear's mother.
6. Little Bear heard a noise and found a mother partridge.
7. Little Bear heard a noise and found Little Sal's mother.
8. Little Sal's mother found little Sal.
9. Little Bear's mother found Little Bear.

Taking It Further . . .

Have each child fold a sheet of drawing paper into fourths. Have children draw one part of the story in each of the four squares and then cut the four squares apart and mix them up. Let students exchange squares with a friend and try to put the squares in order from the event that happened first in the story to the event that happened last.

Blueberries for Sal

Directions: Cut the sentences apart. Glue them on a sheet of drawing paper in the order they happened in the story.

 Little Bear heard a noise and found Little Sal's mother.

 Little Sal's mother found Little Sal.

 Sal and her mother went to pick blueberries.

 Little Bear heard a noise and found a mother partridge.

 Little Bear's mother found Little Bear.

 Little Sal heard a noise and found some crows.

 Sal sat down in a large clump of bushes and ate blueberries.

Little Bear sat down in a large clump of bushes and ate blueberries.

 Little Sal heard a noise and found Little Bear's mother.

Materials:

- worksheet on page 13
- pencils

Lesson Procedure

1. Print the following recipe on the board:

   Blueberry Ice Cream

   2 cups of cream
   1 cup of sugar
   4 eggs
   1 tablespoon of vanilla
   $\frac{1}{2}$ cup blueberries

   Tell the students that this recipe will serve four people. Ask them to change the recipe so that it will serve eight people (4 cups cream, 2 cups sugar, 8 eggs, 2 tablespoons vanilla, 1 cup blueberries). Then have them change the recipe so that it serves only two people (1 cup cream, $\frac{1}{2}$ cup sugar, 2 eggs, $\frac{1}{2}$ tablespoon vanilla, $\frac{1}{4}$ cup blueberries). Challenge students to change the recipe so that it serves ten people (5 cups cream, 2 $\frac{1}{2}$ cups sugar, 10 eggs, 2 $\frac{1}{2}$ tablespoons vanilla, 1 $\frac{1}{4}$ cup blueberries).

2. Pass out the recipe for blueberry waffles. Read over the recipe with the children. Point out that the recipe makes 12 waffles.

3. Have children alter the recipe to make 6, 18, and 24 waffles.

Worksheet Answer Key

	6	18	24
Flour	1 cup	3 cups	4 cups
Baking Powder	1 $\frac{1}{2}$ tsp	4 $\frac{1}{2}$ tsp	6 tsp
Salt	$\frac{3}{8}$ tsp	1 $\frac{1}{8}$ tsp	1 $\frac{1}{2}$ tsp
Milk	1 cup	3 cups	4 cups
Oil	$\frac{1}{4}$ cup	$\frac{3}{4}$ cup	1 cup
Eggs	1	3	4
Vanilla	$\frac{1}{2}$ tsp	1 $\frac{1}{2}$ tsp	2 tsp
Blueberries	$\frac{1}{2}$ cup	1 $\frac{1}{2}$ cups	2 cups

Blueberries for Sal

Blueberry Waffles

Directions: Carefully read the waffle recipe. Then fill in the chart below.

In a large bowl, mix:
   2 cups flour
   3 teaspoons baking powder
   3/4 teaspoon salt

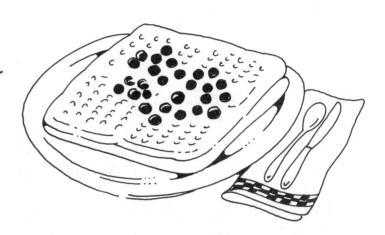

Add and stir in:
   2 cups milk
   1/2 cup oil
   2 egg yolks
   1 teaspoon vanilla

Separately beat two egg whites until stiff. Fold in the beaten egg whites. You will need 1 cup of blueberries. As you pour the batter into the hot waffle iron, sprinkle in some blueberries. (Makes 12 average waffles.)

Supply the correct amounts of each ingredient to make 6, 18, and 24 waffles.

	6	18	24
Flour			
Baking Powder			
Salt			
Milk			
Oil			
Eggs			
Vanilla			
Blueberries			

⚈ • ADDITION & SUBTRACTION FACTS • ⚈

Materials:

• plastic buckets or margarine tubs
• blue beads or marbles for counters*

Lesson Procedure

1. Give each student or group of students a bucket and a supply of blue counters.
2. Reread the first three pages of the book that tell how many berries Sal picked and ate.
3. Present the following math problems to students. Allow them to use the counters to compute the answers.

Sal's mother picked 12 berries. Sal ate 9. How many were left? (3)

Sal picked 15 berries. She ate 4 and dropped 2. How many did she put in her bucket? (9)

Little Bear ate 13 berries off one bush, 5 berries off another bush, and 7 berries off a third bush. How many berries did he eat all together? (25)

Sal ate 9 more berries than Little Bear. Little Bear ate 11 berries. How many berries did Sal eat? (20)

Little Sal's mother filled 4 jars with berries. Each jar could hold 2 cups of berries. How many cups of blueberries did it take to fill all the jars? (8)

Mother Bear ate 8 berries, Little Bear ate 5 berries, and Sal ate 10 berries. How many berries did they eat all together? (23)

Sal's hand could hold 5 blueberries. She reached in her mother's pail and took out 3 handfuls of berries. How many blueberries did she take out of her mother's pail? (15)

Taking It Further . . .

Individually, in pairs, or in small groups, students can make up math problems of their own. Have students exchange problems and solve them.

*Other materials can be used for counters, such as small blue game markers, cotton balls, blue jelly beans, and, of course, blueberries.

Burt Dow,

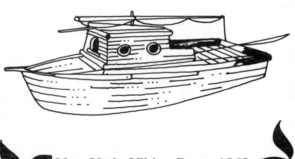

Burt Dow is a practical man. He uses all the leftover paint from his handyman jobs to paint an old boat. He is also a fun-loving man and takes on adventure with inventiveness and humor when he takes his boat out to sea and hooks a whale.

New York: Viking Press, 1963

Deep-Water Man

Materials:

- worksheet on page 17
- pencils

Lesson Procedure

1. Stimulate students to think about the story by discussing these questions:

   What made the story funny?
   What parts of the story were believable and unbelievable?
   What do you know about whales?
   What are some other whale stories?
   What are some other animals that live in or near the sea?

2. List some creative-writing story titles on the board. Ask students to think of some more to add to the list.

   A Whale of a Garage Sale
   How to Fix a Whale
   Whale First Aid
   Burt Dow's Cousin Carl
   Burt Dow, Under-Water Man
   A Whale of a Tale

3. Have each student select a writing topic and write a story or poem on the whale worksheet.

Taking It Further . . .

Have students cut out their whales to make a class book of stories or poems. Make a whale-shaped tagboard cover. Bind the stories and poems with rings or twine.

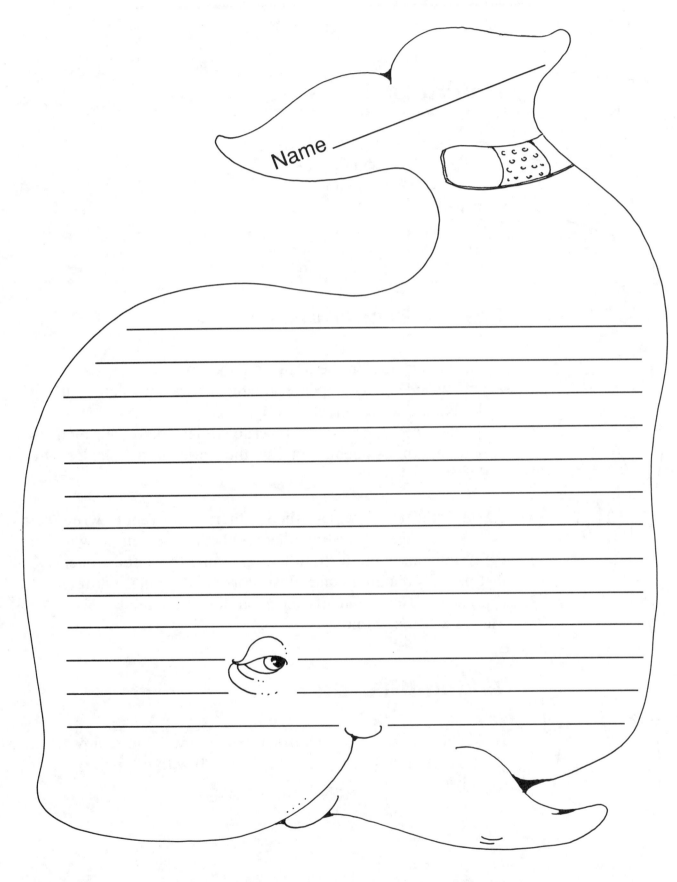

Name

Burt Dow, Deep-Water Man

✧ CREATIVE WRITING ✧

Materials:

- 1" Band-Aids
- 12" x 18" drawing paper
- 8 ¹/₂" x 11" lined paper
- pencils
- crayons or felt pens
- glue

Lesson Procedure

1. Have students fold the drawing paper in half (9" x 12").
2. On one side of the paper, each student draws a picture, using the Band-Aid in a creative way.
3. On the lined paper, students write stories about their pictures.
4. After editing, students can glue the stories to the blank half of the drawing paper.

Some students, like published authors, will want to write their stories before they illustrate them. Others may want to work on the writing and the illustration at the same time. Tell students that published authors and illustrators also use these different approaches. Have students speculate how they think Robert McCloskey did his books.

Taking It Further . . .

Have students brainstorm a list of painless ways to remove a Band-Aid that is stuck (soak in water, rub with oil, pull off quickly).

CREATIVE WRITING

Materials:

- •worksheet on page 20
- •pencils
- •crayons or markers

Lesson Procedure

1. Discuss how Burt Dow painted the Tidely-Idley with leftover paint and how the Tidely-Idley held many memories for Burt.
2. Have students think of things in their homes that hold special memories for them. (My Teddy Bear reminds me of my birthday last year because it was my favorite present.) Have students then think of a color that could represent that memory. (My Teddy Bear is brown.) After ideas have been generated verbally, pass out the worksheet.
3. Have students color the boards on the boat with different colors that bring back memories. On the lines provided, have students explain what memories the colors represent. (The blue reminds me of the back porch where my Dad reads to me after dinner. The yellow reminds me of the wallpaper on my bedroom walls. The white reminds me of our picket fence. I helped paint it.)
4. Primary students will usually stick to concrete examples. Encourage older students to use the colors to represent feelings or more abstract memories. (The red is for the embarrassment I felt when I fell out of the boat the first time I went water-skiing.)

Taking It Further . . .

Discuss Burt Dow's practical use of leftover paint. Provide leftover art supplies (scraps of paper, small amounts of paint, broken crayons, and used magazines). Students can draw boats or pictures of their choices and decorate them with the leftover supplies.

Color Memories

Directions: Color the boards on the boat with colors that bring back memories. On the lines, explain what memories the colors remind you of.

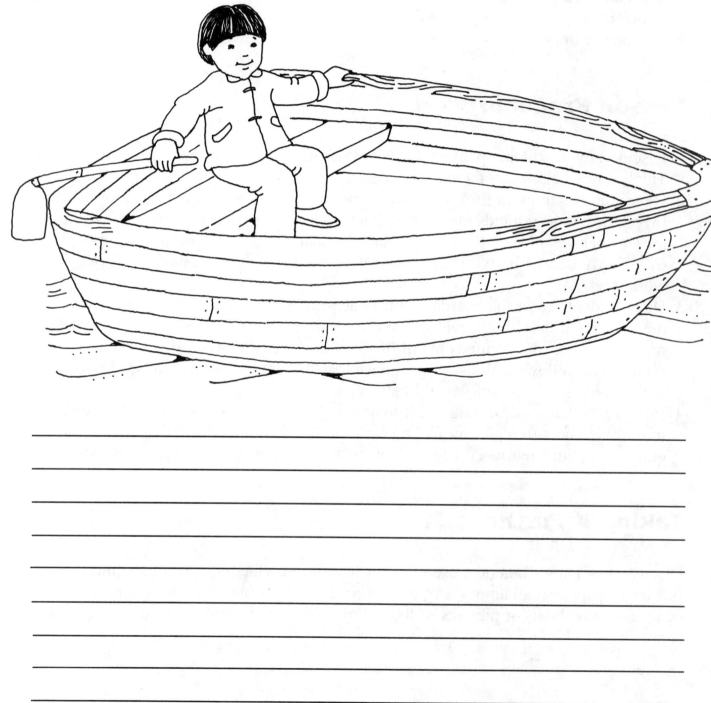

_____

_____

_____

_____

_____

_____

_____

The Robert McCloskey Connection © 1990 Fearon Teacher Aids

MATH COMPUTATION

Materials:

Lesson Procedure

1. Together, count the whales in the story. Count the Band-Aids.
2. Provide students with problems to solve based on the story.

Counting:
How many whales are there on pages 56 and 57? (11)

Adding:
How many pink whales? (3)
How many lime-green whales? (2)
How many pink and green whales all together? (5)

Subtracting:
How many whales? (11)
How many Band-Aids on whales? (4)
How many whales are left without Band-Aids? (7)

Multiplying:
How many Band-Aids would be needed if each whale wanted 3 Band-Aids? (33)
If each whale wanted 4? (44)
If each whale wanted 7? (77)

Division:
If Burt had a box of 180 Band-Aids, how many would each whale get? (16)
How many would be left? (4)

Taking It Further . . .

Primary students can use Band-Aids as counters for math problems. Older students can do research to estimate the weight of one whale, two whales, six whales; the speed of the Tidely-Idley; and the distance that Burt Dow traveled.

Materials:

- •drawing paper
- •crayons or markers
- •pencils
- •first-aid manual or health text

Lesson Procedure

1. Have students share experiences they have had administering first aid to someone in need. Discuss some simple first-aid procedures (washing a cut and covering it with a sterile dressing or applying ice to a swollen area after a blow).
2. Remind students how Burt Dow took the hook out of the whale's tail. He "snipped off the barb and eased out the hook." Then he put a Band-Aid on the tail. Discuss with the students whether he did the right thing.
3. Divide the class into groups of three to six. Assign each group a different first-aid rule or topic from a health text or Red Cross manual, such as:
   a. Apply direct pressure to a bleeding cut.
   b. Do not move a victim who may have a broken bone.
   c. Make sure the victim has an open airway.
   d. Warm a shock victim by placing blankets over and under the body.
   e. Place a sterile dressing over an open wound.
   f. To treat first- and second-degree burns, place the injured area in cool water to relieve the pain.
   g. Use the Heimlich maneuver to remove an object from a choking victim.
4. Have students draw pictures of their first-aid information, using whale illustrations.
5. Bind all reports into a class book, entitled *First-Aid Manual for Whales*. This is an excellent method for reviewing a first-aid unit.

Taking It Further . . .

Reproduce pages from the *First-Aid Manual for Whales* on transparencies or slides for a parent program.

❧ SELF-CONCEPT ❧

Materials:

•worksheet on page 24
•pencils

Lesson Procedure

1. Burt Dow was a happy man. Discuss with the students why they think he was happy. (He had hobbies. He was himself. He helped others. He took his time.)
2. Let students share things that make them happy.
3. Pass out the "Happiness Inventory." Have students list things in their lives that make them happy.

Taking It Further . . .

Discuss things that people can do to make their lives happier. Discuss things over which people have control and things over which they do not have control. Have students write personal happiness goals. Set a date when the "Happiness Inventory" will be repeated. Encourage students to work on their goals. On the planned date (three to four weeks later), repeat the "Happiness Inventory." Discuss how this inventory compares with the first and how we can have control over our own happiness.

Happiness Inventory

Burt Dow was happy because . . .

_____

_____

_____

_____

_____

_____

_____

I am happy because . . .

_____

_____

_____

_____

_____

_____

_____

_____

Burt Dow, Deep-Water Man

The Robert McCloskey Connection © 1990 Fearon Teacher Aids

Journey

Johnny had a happy home with Merry and Grumble, until Grumble announced that their tiny farm could no longer support the three of them. Johnny packed up his few belongings and a journey cake from Merry and headed out for a new place to work and live. Author and illustrator both use characterization, exaggeration, and repetition to create a warm and entertaining story of a boy who finds his way back home.

Written by Ruth Sawyer
New York: Viking Press, 1953

Cake, Ho!

DRAWING

Materials:

- •worksheets on pages 27–29
- •drawing paper
- •pencils
- •crayons or markers (optional)

Lesson Procedure

1. Make a list on the board as students name all of the animals mentioned in the story:

Raucus, the crow	pig
cow	chicken
duck	donkey
sheep	

2. On the chalkboard, overhead projector, or large piece of butcher paper, demonstrate how to draw one of the animals, using the step-by-step illustrations.
3. Pass out the worksheets and drawing paper. Have students draw the farm animals.

Taking It Further . . .

The worksheets can be placed in a study center with the following directions:

1. Take one worksheet at a time.
2. Draw the two animals on your own paper.
3. Write a story about your two animals.
4. Have a friend help you edit your story.

Cow

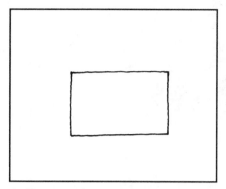

1. Draw a box.

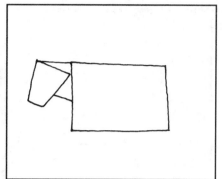

2. Draw a head and neck.

3. Add a face.

4. Draw a leg and udder.

5. Draw three more legs.

6. Add spots and a tail.

Duck

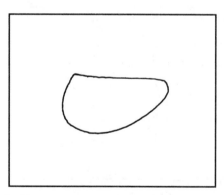

1. Draw a pear.

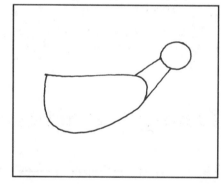

2. Add a neck.

3. Draw a head.

4. Draw a bill and eyes.

5. Add a tail.

6. Draw feet.

Sheep

1. Draw a cloud.

2. Draw a *U* for the head.

3. Draw a face.

4. Add a tail.

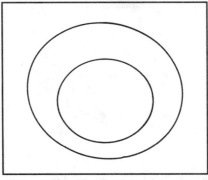

5. Draw four legs.

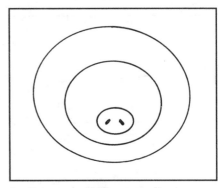

6. Add some grass.

Pig

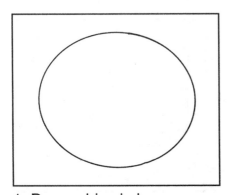

1. Draw a big circle.

2. Draw a medium circle.

3. Draw a nose.

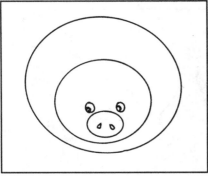

4. Add eyes.

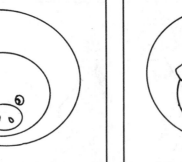

5. Draw two ears.

6. Draw a tail and make two *W*'s for feet.

The Robert McCloskey Connection © 1990 Fearon Teacher Aids

Journey Cake, Ho!

Hen

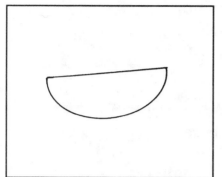

1. Draw a falling *D*.

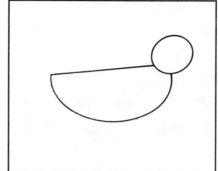

2. Add a head.

3. Draw a face.

4. Draw two *U*'s for legs.

5. Draw *Y*'s for feet.

6. Add a tail and wings.

Donkey

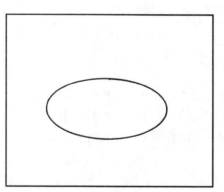

1. Draw a watermelon.

2. Add a neck and head.

3. Draw a face.

4. Draw a mane and tail.

5. Add four legs.

6. Draw four feet.

EARLY AMERICAN PROJECTS

Materials:

•supplies will vary, depending on the project students choose

Lesson Procedure

1. Have students recall the jobs that each character in the story did. Write the jobs on the chalkboard under the appropriate headings.

Merry	Grumble	Johnny
card wool	tend garden	split kindling
spin wool	shear sheep	fill wood box
laid the fire	milk cow	lug water
tend the griddle	fell trees	feed creatures
churn butter	saw logs	fish
sing	grumble	whistle

Other early American jobs or crafts could be added to the list:

make candles	quilt	whittle
make reed whistles	make cornhusk dolls	make scarecrows

2. Students select projects to complete in the classroom during the next few weeks.
3. Students are responsible for researching directions and collecting materials. It is often possible to recruit parents, grandparents, and people from the community to demonstrate and teach crafts to the students.

Taking It Further . . .

Primary students can do simple class activities, such as the following:
•Churn butter (Merry): Put cream in a baby food jar. Have students shake until it turns to butter. Pour out whey.
•Plant miniature gardens (Grumble): Have students plant seeds or small plants in milk cartons that have been cut in half.
•Make fishing poles (Johnny): Students tie magnets to string, which they tie to sticks. Then they make and fish for paper fish that have paper clips attached.

VOCABULARY

Materials:

Lesson Procedure

1. Discuss with the children some of the unfamiliar terms in the book. Explain their meanings or the history behind them.

   Pages 6–7 "There were three of them: the old woman, Merry; the old man, Grumble; and Johnny, the *bound-out* boy."
   In Colonial America, children of poor families were apprenticed to learn a trade while living with and serving a master. Sometimes, children, especially girls, were "bound-out" by their parents as household servants in exchange for room and board.
   Page 8 "The old woman took care of the wool; she *carded* and spun and knit it."
   The process of carding wool was done prior to spinning. It consisted of cleaning, untangling, and collecting fibers together.
   Page 9 "Ho, for a *Journey Cake*—Quick on a griddle bake!"
   A Johnny Cake is a bread made with cornmeal. The name was altered in the story because of the "journey" the cake took Johnny on in his chase.
   Page 11 "Life's a *nettlesome* thing."
   Nettlesome is a synonym for irritating.
   Page 15 "On the tallest tree sat Raucus, the *sentinel* crow. . . ."
   Sentinel is an adjective derived from the noun, sentry. A sentry is a soldier standing guard at a point of passage.
   Page 40 "I'm all of a *tucker!*"
   Related to the expression "tuckered out," meaning exhausted.

2. Encourage students to try using these words in a sentence of their own. Ask them what they consider to be nettlesome or what it takes to tucker them out.

Taking It Further . . .

Discuss the practice of apprenticeships and being *bound-out*. Ask students to think of advantages and disadvantages. Discuss other literature with examples of apprentices (*Johnny Tremain*). Discuss trades or professions students could learn through an apprenticeship. Write "contracts" describing the apprenticeships students might try.

CHORAL READING

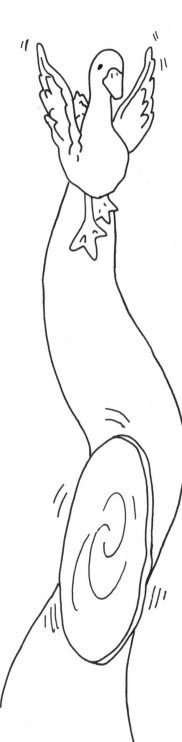

Materials:

Lesson Procedure

1. Instruct students to listen for the names of animals in the story as you read it the first time.
2. After reading, list the animals on the board.

cow	pig	donkey
duck	hen	journey cake
sheep		

3. Reread the story, "conducting" the groups to read their parts chorally as you get to them. Have the class compose words for the sheep, the pig, and the hens.

Journey Cake:
"Journey Cake, ho!
Journey Cake, hi!
Catch me and eat me
As I roll by!"

Cow:
"At running I'll beat you.
I'll catch you and eat you!"

Duck:
"At flying I'll beat you.
I'll catch and I'll eat you!"

Donkey:
"I'll show you I can beat you.
I'll catch you and eat you."

Taking It Further . . .

Recreate the story by combining words of two or three groups at a time (pigs and chickens or ducks and sheep). Encourage students to use high, low, fast, and slow voices. Produce choral or puppet performances, using "The Gingerbread Boy" or similar stories.

MATH COMPUTATION

Materials:

•lined paper
•pencils

Lesson Procedure

1. List all the animals from the story on the board.
2. Have the students put them in order from the one they think weighs the least to the one they think weighs the most. Then assign weights to each animal. Students can estimate or you can provide the information.

crow (2 lbs)	fox (11 lbs)	pig (300 lbs)
hen (6 lbs)	wolf (80 lbs)	donkey (700 lbs)
duck (8 lbs)	sheep (200 lbs)	cow (900 lbs)

3. Create math problems using the information given, and have the students compute the answers.
   a. How much would the hen and the duck weigh together? (14 lbs)
   b. How much more does the donkey weigh than the wolf? (620 lbs)
   c. If a truck could hold only 1,000 pounds, how many pigs could fit in the truck without exceeding the weight limit? (3)
   d. If a cow were on one end of a teeter-totter, how many pigs would it take on the other end to make it balance? (3)
   e. Which would weigh more, four sheep or three pigs? (3 pigs)

Taking It Further . . .

Primary children can use plastic toy animals or color-coded manipulatives when working problems. Older students can make bar graphs to represent the weights of the animals.

INTERDEPENDENCE

Materials:

- worksheet on page 35
- pencils

Lesson Procedure

1. Discuss the interdependence of Merry, Grumble, and Johnny as it relates to the jobs they did. Johnny fed the cow, Grumble milked the cow, and Merry used the milk to make butter. Discuss how people need one another.
2. Reread the two poems in the story in which Merry and Grumble told about their work.
3. Give students a chance to fill in the worksheet and tell a little about the jobs they do at home.

Taking It Further . . .

Challenge students to write poems about the work they do at home or school. Tell them to emphasize their feelings about those jobs. Encourage a variety of poetry styles: couplet, quatrain, limerick, or haiku.

Name _____

Everyone Has a Job

List the jobs each character in the story had to do.

Merry: _____

_____

_____

_____

Grumble: _____

_____

_____

_____

Johnny: _____

_____

_____

_____

Make a list of jobs you do at home or at school:

_____

_____

_____

_____

_____

_____

_____

_____

Materials:

- •worksheet on page 37
- •pencils
- •book of names and their meanings (optional)

Lesson Procedure

1. Discuss with the children the significance of the names Merry and Grumble. Ask if the names were appropriate and why.
2. Discuss students' names. Let students share stories that relate to how they got their names. If you have a book with names and meanings, look up several students' names.
3. Have students complete the worksheet.

Taking It Further . . .

When students go home, have them ask their parents about their names and share any new information they have learned with the class the next day.

Journey Cake, Ho!

What's in a Name?

1. What is your name? _____
2. Tell any information you know about what your name means or why your parents named you as they did.

_____

_____

3. If you could change your name, what would you like it to be? Why?

_____

_____

4. If you were given a name based on one of your personality traits or attitudes, what do you think your name might be? (Be honest!)

_____

_____

5. Tell what personality trait or attitude you would **like** to be known for, and tell what name you would have.

_____

_____

_____

Lentil

Lentil could not whistle or sing. So, he learned to play the harmonica. He took his harmonica everywhere, even to welcome the town's hero, Colonel Carter. A delightful slice of Americana.

WELCOME Colonel Carter

New York: Viking Press, 1940

WHITTLING

Materials:

- knives
- pieces of soft wood (pieces of pine or cedar two-by-fours work well)
- drawing paper
- pencils

Lesson Procedure

1. Discuss what whittling is with the class. Show examples, if available. Explain to students that whittling developed as a means to pass the time, using materials that were naturally available. Ask students what kinds of things Old Sneep could have whittled.
2. Have students think about what they would like to whittle. Encourage them to keep it simple. Some suggestions might include a geometric shape or a block letter from the students' names. Have students sketch their ideas before they begin to whittle.
3. This project is best done with older children, and it is recommended that you have adult helpers to supervise. Discuss knife safety with the students before they begin whittling.

Taking It Further . . .

Whittling cannot be done with anything other than wood because that is what whittling is. However, younger children can carve materials such as soap, vegetables, styrofoam, or plaster of Paris, using a blunt knife.

CREATIVE WRITING

Materials:

•worksheet on page 42
•pencils

Lesson Procedure

1. See if children can recall all of the places Lentil played his harmonica. Then list them on the board.

    bathtub (his favorite place)
    down Vine Street past the finest house in Alto
    past the drugstore
    past the barbershop
    past the library
    by the Methodist Church
    through the park
    at the welcome ceremony for Colonel Carter

2. Give students a copy of the worksheet. Then give them three minutes to think of as many places as possible to play a harmonica. The purpose of this assignment is to develop fluency and creativity. Encourage the students to brainstorm and write down whatever comes to their minds.

3. When the time is up, have students read over their lists and choose three ideas they consider the most creative and original to share with the class.

Taking It Further . . .

Lentil played in the bathtub because he thought the tone was "one hundred percent better." Have students choose one of their ideas and develop it into a paragraph telling why that would be a good place to play a harmonica.

Where Can You Play a Harmonica?

Directions: Write down as many places that you can think of to play a harmonica. (Lentil especially liked playing in the bathtub!)

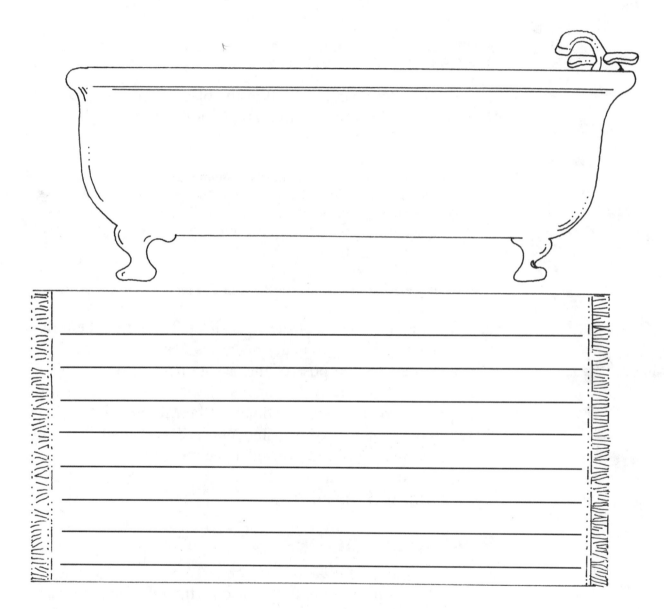

Add more on the back.

The Robert McCloskey Connection © 1990 Fearon Teacher Aids

Lentil

CREATIVE WRITING

Materials:

•lined paper
•pencils

Lesson Procedure

1. Write the first verse of "She'll Be Comin' 'Round the Mountain" on the board.

   She'll be comin' 'round the mountain when she comes (toot, toot),
   She'll be comin' 'round the mountain when she comes (toot, toot),
   She'll be comin' 'round the mountain, she'll be comin' 'round the
      mountain, she'll be comin' 'round the mountain when she comes
      (toot, toot).

2. Compose new verses with the class, relating to something that happened in the story.

   He'll be sitting in the bathtub when he plays (bwah! bwah!), or
   He'll be eating sour lemons on the roof (slurp! slurp!).

3. Have students compose some original verses of their own.
4. Try singing several new verses together.

Taking It Further . . .

Have students illustrate their verses on sheets of drawing paper and staple them together in a class songbook.

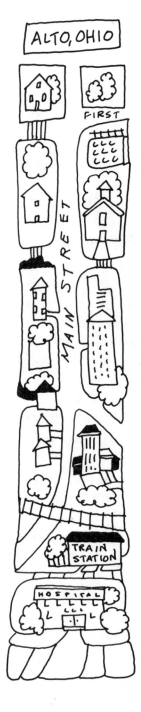

Materials:

- •drawing paper
- •pencils

Lesson Procedure

1. On the chalkboard, list all the information the book gives about Alto, Ohio.

   There was a Main Street with a beautiful big house on it.
   There was a drugstore, barbershop, and library.
   There was a Methodist Church and a park.
   There was an alley behind the hardware store.
   There was a train station.
   A new hospital was going to be built.

2. Pass out the white drawing paper. Have students design a map of Alto, Ohio, including all of the buildings and streets mentioned. They can add their own ideas as well.

Taking It Further . . .

Make a tabletop model of Alto, Ohio. Have students bring in various sizes of boxes that they can paint and decorate to resemble buildings. Draw streets and add other details. Let students be creative. Let them work on the city when they have free time between assignments until it is completed.

SELF-CONCEPT

Materials:

• worksheet on page 46
• pencils

Lesson Procedure

1. Discuss with the children how Lentil compensated for his inability to whistle and sing by learning to play the harmonica.
2. Pass out the worksheet. Have students list what they consider to be their weaknesses or things they cannot do in the "whistle" column. Have them list their talents or the activities they could learn to do in the "harmonica" column.
3. At the bottom of the page, help students set a realistic goal for themselves of something they can learn to do within one month (play a new song on the piano, bake cookies, say the alphabet backward, memorize a poem, count to twenty in French, juggle, or do the splits). Be sure to set a goal for yourself also!

Taking It Further . . .

After the month's time, check up on the students and see if they reached their goals. Plan to have a celebration day so that students can demonstrate what they have learned to do.

Name _____

Directions: Make a list of things you consider difficult to do in the "whistle" column. List your talents in the "harmonica" column. At the bottom of the page, set a realistic goal of something you can learn to do in one month.

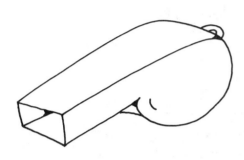 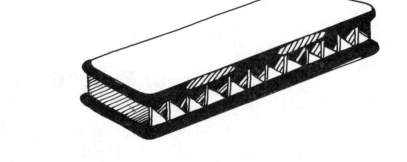

Things I think are difficult . . .   My talents . . .

_____   _____

_____   _____

_____   _____

_____   _____

_____   _____

_____   _____

_____   _____

Goal:

_____

_____

_____

_____

The Robert McCloskey Connection © 1990 Fearon Teacher Aids

Lentil

Make Way

Mr. and Mrs. Mallard are looking for a place to raise a family. Boston and the Public Garden seem unlikely, but there are the swan boats, and there is Michael, who feeds them peanuts. McCloskey's ability to dip into the heart of human sharing has made this book a classic for all children.

New York: Viking Press, 1941

for Ducklings

☙ • COTTON BALL DUCKLING • ☙

Materials:

For each student:
- two yellow cotton balls or cosmetic puffs*
- 2" squares of orange construction paper for bill and feet
- 2" squares of white and black construction paper for eyes
- 6" piece of yarn
- scissors
- white glue

Lesson Procedure

1. Draw a sketch on the board of the cotton ball duckling. Explain how the craft items should be cut and glued together.
2. Pass out supplies and allow students to make ducklings. Encourage originality. Remind the students that each duckling will have its own personality.
3. A group of children can name their ducklings by following the alphabetical pattern in the book.

Taking It Further . . .

Other cotton ball critters can be created with a little imagination. They make nice Christmas tree ornaments around the holidays, or a magnet can be glued on the back to make a refrigerator friend.

*Yellow cosmetic puffs can be purchased in the cosmetic department of many stores. If not available, yellow puffs can be made by shaking white puffs in a bag of powdered, yellow tempera paint.

Make Way for Ducklings

ADJECTIVES

Materials:

•worksheet on page 50
•pencils

Lesson Procedure

1. See if the children can name all of the ducklings (Jack, Kack, Lack, Mack, Nack, Ouack, Pack, and Quack). Help students notice that the names are in alphabetical order using the letters J through Q. Discuss characteristics of the different ducklings.
2. Have students write one adjective on each shell of the worksheet to describe the ducklings. Some suggestions may have been mentioned when you discussed the characteristics of the ducklings (fluffy, soft, small, curious, yellow, newborn, energetic, eager, obedient, noisy).
3. Invite children to color the ducklings when they have written an adjective on each shell.

Taking It Further . . .

Have students write a story from the perspective of one of the ducklings. Have them describe how they felt when crossing the street with their mother and all the cars were honking, what they thought of the big swan, or how they like peanuts.

Adjectives

Directions: Write one adjective that describes the ducklings on each shell.

Make Way for Ducklings

VERBS

Materials:

- lined paper
- pencils

Lesson Procedure

1. Have children name as many things as possible that ducks do and list them on the chalkboard (fly, flap, fish, quack, waddle, eat, dive, peck, swim, wade, walk, drink).
2. Discuss the word list on the board. Remind students that words naming things we do are called verbs (action words). Ask students if there are any words in the list on the board that are not verbs. Erase those words from the list.
3. Have students use the verb list as a word bank for creative writing. Instruct students to create a story using a variety of expressive verbs.

Taking It Further . . .

Write each verb on a 3" x 5" card. Divide the class into teams or partners to play charades. Stack all the cards in one pile face down. One player looks at the top card and acts it out while the partner or team tries to guess what verb is on the card. Repeat until all cards have been guessed.

ENVIRONMENTS

Materials:

•lined paper
•pencils

Lesson Procedure

1. Discuss the options for homes the Mallards considered and the dangers that were presented by each one.

   The woods had foxes and there were sure to be turtles in the water.
   In the Public Garden, a bicycle nearly ran over them.
   Louisburg Square had no water to swim in.

2. Have students contribute as you make a list of wild animals on the board.
3. Have students each select a different animal and write the name of the animal at the top of their papers.
4. Have students fold the paper in half lengthwise to make two columns separated by the fold line. Give the students four minutes to list criteria for a good home for their animals in the left column.
5. Give students four more minutes to list possible homesites for their animals in the column on the right.
6. Using information from both lists, students can write paragraphs describing ideal homes for their animals on a second sheet of paper.

Taking It Further . . .

Encourage students to build models of different animal habitats, using shoe boxes or terrariums.

BOSTON HISTORY

Materials:

- lined paper
- pencils
- encyclopedias
- reference books

Lesson Procedure

1. On the chalkboard, list features of Boston that are referred to in the book (Public Garden and swan boats, Beacon Hill, State House, Louisburg Square, Charles River, Mount Vernon Street, Old Corner Bookstore, Charles Street, and Beacon Street).
2. Encourage older children to contribute to a list of people, places, and historical events relative to Boston.

People: Louisa May Alcott, William Blackstone, Ralph Waldo Emerson, William Lloyd Garrison, Nathaniel Hawthorne, Henry Wadsworth Longfellow, Paul Revere, and John Winthrop.

Places: Faneuil Hall, Old South Meetinghouse, Park Street Church, King's Chapel, Paul Revere's House, and Old North Church.

Events:

1615–1617	measle and scarlet fever epidemic
1620s	William Blackstone built cottage on Beacon Hill
1630	a group of 800 Puritans led by John Winthrop founded Charlestown
1632	Boston became the capital of Massachusetts Bay Colony
1635	Boston Latin School established (first American public school)
1765	Stamp Act
1770	Boston Massacre
1773	Boston Tea Party
1775	Battles of Lexington, Concord, and Bunker Hill
1776	Declaration of Independence
1783	end of the Revolutionary War
1822	Boston chartered as a city
1840s	Irish immigration
1872	Boston fire
1897	nation's first subway

3. In groups of three to four, students select historical people, places, or events and write reports about them. Have primary students draw simple maps of Boston, locating the features mentioned in the book.

Taking It Further . . .

On one set of 3" x 5" cards, write the historical dates from page 53. On another set of 3" x 5" cards, write the events. Mix the cards and pass one out to each student. One at a time, students read their cards while other students listen for a match.

For primary children, write the historical date on half of a 3" x 5" card and write the event on the other half of the card. Pass out the cards and have students read them aloud to the class. Instruct everyone to listen carefully because the next game will test their memories. After all cards have been read, collect the cards, cut them in half, and redistribute the halves. On a signal, see if students can find a partner whose card matches theirs. Try playing the game by matching authors and books (Louisa May Alcott, *Little Women*; Henry Wadsworth Longfellow, *Hiawatha*) or names and sayings (Paul Revere, "One if by land, two if by sea.")

MAPPING

Materials:

- •drawing paper
- •pencils
- •crayons or markers

Lesson Procedure

1. Make a list on the board as students recall the features of Boston described in the book.

   woods
   pond in Public Garden with a little island on it
   Beacon Hill
   State House
   Louisburg Square
   Police Headquarters
   Corner Book Shop
   Charles River
   Mount Vernon Street
   Charles Street
   Beacon Street

2. Have students draw city maps in pencil that include all of the features mentioned.
3. When the maps are complete, students can color them with crayons or markers.

Taking It Further . . .

Make a gameboard, using the features of Boston listed in the book. Draw squares around the edges of the paper. Label squares with the names of places and streets in Boston. Blank squares indicate a player must draw a card. Cards can say such things as: "Traffic, lose one turn," or "Michael helps out, move ahead 3 spaces." The first person to make it all the way around town is the winner. Older students can do research to locate actual city maps of Boston.

✦ INTERDEPENDENCE ✦

Materials:

Lesson Procedure

1. Discuss with the children how the Mallards each had a job to do and how other people helped them. Mr. Mallard scouted the area, Mrs. Mallard trained the ducklings, and Michael fed them peanuts and stopped traffic.
2. Discuss how each student (and the teacher) is needed in the classroom. Some students are needed for their friendliness and sportsmanship, others for their math or reading skills, others for creative ideas, and others because of their calm dispositions.

Taking It Further . . .

Relate the concept of interdependence to classroom jobs. If you don't already have classroom assistants, have the students help make a list of classroom jobs that need to be done. Use library book pockets to make a work chart. Let each student or group of students decorate a pocket by drawing their favorite part from the story. Attach the pockets to a large posterboard. Write the students' names on 3" x 5" cards. Use the cards to assign weekly jobs.

☙ HEALTH AND SAFETY RULES ☙

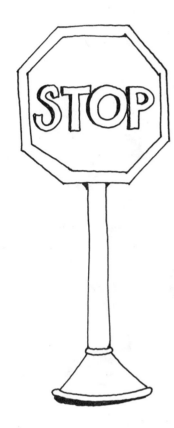

Materials:

- worksheets on pages 58, 59, or 60
- pencils
- crayons or markers

Lesson Procedure

1. Discuss some of the dangers the Mallards faced (being hit by a bicycle or car). Ask children to share warnings their parents have given them (walk on the right side of the street, cross at corners). Discuss some safety rules Mrs. Mallard might have told the ducklings to follow (walk in line, watch out for things with wheels, come home when called).
2. Divide the class into three groups. Have students write safety rules to remember when riding a bike, swimming, or crossing traffic, depending on the worksheet you give them. Students can work individually or in groups.

Taking It Further . . .

Have each child choose one rule and illustrate it to make a safety poster.

Bicycle Safety Rules

Directions: Write down as many bicycle safety rules as you can.

_____

_____

_____

_____

_____

_____

_____

_____

_____

Make Way for Ducklings

Traffic Safety Rules

Directions: Write down as many traffic safety rules as you can.

_____

_____

_____

_____

_____

_____

_____

_____

_____

_____

Swimming Safety Rules

Directions: Write down as many swimming safety rules as you can.

_____

_____

_____

_____

_____

_____

_____

_____

_____

_____

The Robert McCloskey Connection © 1990 Fearon Teacher Aids

Make Way for Ducklings

One

While Sal was helping her father dig clams, she lost her first loose tooth in the muddy gravel. She worried that a clam would get the wish intended for her. *One Morning in Maine* could be any morning, anywhere. McCloskey makes what seems commonplace important for readers of all ages.

New York: Viking Press, 1952

Morning in Maine

CREATIVE WRITING

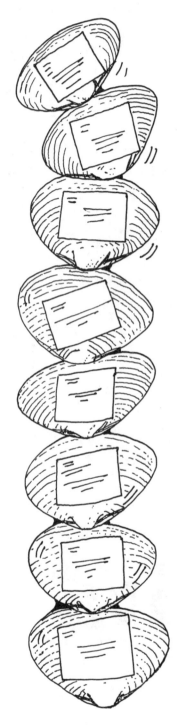

Materials:

- •paper clams*
- •lined paper
- •pencils
- •plastic or metal bucket

Lesson Procedure

1. Before beginning the lesson, write a story idea on each of the paper clams. Use the suggestions below, or use your own ideas. Story ideas can be repeated on several clams. Students enjoy hearing different treatments of the same idea. Fold the clams and put them in the bucket.

   One Time When I Clammed Up
   If I Were a Clam
   20 Ways to Use a Clam Shell
   A Day at the Beach
   Two Clams Meet for the First Time

2. Pass around the clam bucket and let each student choose one clam. Have students write stories based on the ideas written inside their clams.

Taking It Further . . .

After editing, mount clam stories on giant sheets of colored clam-shaped paper. Display on a bulletin board or bind the giant clams together in a class book.

*To make paper clams, fold colored paper (3" x 6") in half. Trace a circle with the edge on the fold. Cut out the double circle with pinking shears, leaving a section of fold for a hinge. Make one for each student.

CREATIVE WRITING

Materials:

- •feathers
- •lined paper
- •pencils

Lesson Procedure

1. Remind students that in the story, Sal picks up a sea gull feather to make a wish on, after she loses her tooth in the muddy gravel. She begins to think that anything that is taken out or falls out is something on which a wish can be made. Encourage discussion among students about what they might wish for if they were granted three wishes.
2. Pass out three feathers to each student. Use sea gull feathers if available. Other options include feathers from craft stores, paper feathers, and rubbings of feathers.
3. Have students write one wish for each feather on a sheet of paper and glue or tape the feathers beside the wishes.

Taking It Further . . .

Make a wish box. Fill it with small prizes. When students lose teeth, let them draw a prize out of the wish box. Or, for fluency and creative thinking, have students make a list of things on which wishes can be made (wishbone, four-leaf clover). Allow them to add new possibilities to the list (spark plug, gold cars).

❧• CREATIVE THINKING •❧

Materials:

- worksheet on page 65
- lined paper
- pencils

Lesson Procedure

1. Sal hoped that her secret wish for a chocolate ice-cream cone would come true. Give each student a chance to tell his or her favorite flavor of ice cream.
2. Divide students into groups of four to six.
3. Instruct the groups to select a secretary and list as many flavors of ice cream (real or imaginary) as they can in three minutes.
4. At the end of the three minutes, the groups identify five of their most unusual flavors ("No other group would think of these.") Each group chooses a spokesperson to read the list to the class.
5. Give groups two additional minutes to add to their lists.
6. Hand out the worksheets. Students color each scoop to represent a different flavor and label it.

Taking It Further . . .

Instead of using the worksheet, have each group use a large piece of butcher paper and design a gigantic five-scoop ice-cream cone!

Directions: Color each scoop and give it a name. Cut the scoops out and connect them together to make one huge ice-cream cone.

One Morning in Maine

❧ • COUNTING MONEY • ❧

Materials:

•lined paper
•pencils

Lesson Procedure

1. Make up math problems, using information in the story.

  If Sal sold clams for $.10 each and she sold 23 clams, how much money
  would she earn? ($2.30)

  If Sal had 23 clams in her bucket and she sold 14, how many would she
  have left? (9) How much money would she earn? ($1.40)

  The repair bill for the boat motor was $7.50. Sal's father gave Mr.
  Condon a ten-dollar bill. How much change did he get back? ($2.50)

  If ice cream is $.75 a scoop, how much would you pay for three
  scoops? ($2.25)

2. Have the students create new problems to challenge each
   other.

Taking It Further . . .

Use play money to act out the math problems suggested by
the story.

ANIMAL STUDIES

Materials:

Lesson Procedure

1. See if children can name all the animals, sea creatures, or birds mentioned in the story. List them on the chalkboard.

   Penny the dog
   cat (pictured but not mentioned)
   fish hawk
   loon
   seal
   sea gulls
   mussels
   clams

2. After the list is made, discuss which animals have teeth and which do not. For the animals without teeth, see if children can give a possible reason why.
3. Discuss ways animals acquire their food, eat their food, and what food they eat.

Taking It Further . . .

Have students select different animals and report on their food and eating habits.

COMMUNITY COMPARISONS

Materials:

- •butcher paper
- •crayons or markers

Lesson Procedure

1. Discuss the community in Maine as it is described in the book.

   People there traveled by boat.
   There was a small general store.
   Everyone knows everyone else.

2. Discuss your community. Compare it to the one in Maine.
3. On butcher paper, make a chart comparing different kinds of communities (communities the children have lived in or communities described in other books). Label the communities across the top and list categories down the side (travel, shopping, housing, population, leisure time, and jobs). Fill in the chart as you discuss the various communities.

Taking It Further . . .

Design your classroom to represent a community. Label the four walls North, East, South, and West. Label aisles as streets. Designate different areas to represent the library, post office, grocery store, and other points of interest.

Time

Time of Wonder is a wonder itself, awakening all of the senses to life around us. Listen to a million splashes as the rain falls. Watch the beach disappear in the fog. Feel the force of a summer storm. Experience one special summer on an island in Maine.

New York: Viking Press, 1957

# of Wonder

CREATING MOOD

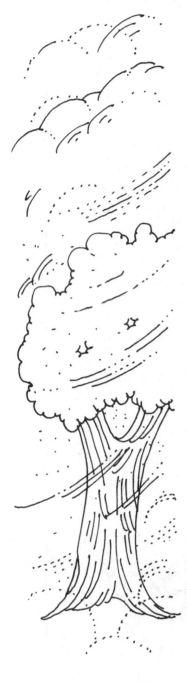

Materials:

- drawing paper
- tissue paper
- crayons or markers

Lesson Procedure

1. Show children the pictures in the book on pages 12–17, which vividly portray fog-covered surroundings. Contrast the fog in these pictures with the clarity of pages 19–21, when the fog has lifted.
2. Ask students to think of ways to create a foggy scene (chalk, smudging the picture, watercolor wash).
3. Demonstrate how placing a thin piece of white tissue paper over an illustration from the book can create the illusion of fog.
4. Have students draw pictures of outdoor settings with crayons or markers. Let them experiment with creating fog by placing tissue paper over the pictures when completed.

Taking It Further . . .

Let children experiment with other methods for creating fog.

❦ SIMILES AND METAPHORS ❦

Materials:

- worksheet on page 72
- pencils

Lesson Procedure

1. Discuss McCloskey's use of descriptive language.

   A simile is a figure of speech that compares two unlike things and is usually introduced by the word "as" or "like." On page 14, McCloskey writes, "Back from the shore the trees look like ghosts."

   A metaphor is an implied comparison between two usually unrelated things. A metaphor does not use the words "like" or "as" to make the comparison. On page 28 we read, "In the quiet of the night one hundred pairs of eyes are watching you." McCloskey uses this metaphor to describe the stars.

2. Hand out the worksheet. Have students think of other examples of similes and metaphors to describe the stars (little lanterns in the sky, holes in the sky, tiny flashlights, sugar sprinkled on black velvet).

3. After students have had time to work independently, encourage them to share their ideas, and list them on the chalkboard.

Taking It Further . . .

Have each student choose a favorite simile or metaphor and write it in a complete sentence on a strip of white paper. Students then glue the strips of white paper on the bottom of sheets of black or blue construction paper. Have them add stars, using gold star stickers, white chalk, yellow crayons, or glitter. Bind all the pictures together to make a class book.

Name _____

Directions: List as many similes and metaphors as you can think of to describe the stars.

Similes   Metaphors

_____   _____
_____   _____
_____   _____
_____   _____
_____   _____
_____   _____
_____   _____
_____   _____
_____   _____
_____   _____
_____   _____

The Robert McCloskey Connection © 1990 Fearon Teacher Aids

Time of Wonder

❧ • MONEY • ❧

Materials:

- catalogs, grocery ads, sales tabloids
- lined paper
- pencils

Lesson Procedure

1. Discuss provisions the family needed on Deer Island:

    groceries
    gasoline
    anchors
    rope
    chain
    games

2. Divide the class into groups of four to six. Tell the groups that they must work within a specific budget (predetermined by you) to "purchase" the needed supplies.
3. Provide students with catalogs, grocery ads, and sales tabloids to determine prices. For younger children, provide more specific lists and prices.
4. Emphasize decision-making skills (listing criteria, trade-offs, and prioritizing).

Taking It Further . . .

Have students use the telephone directory yellow pages to locate places to purchase 2" rope, 1" chain, and a Parcheesi game.

☙· SCIENTIFIC OBSERVATION ·☙

Materials:

•worksheet on page 75
•pencils

Lesson Procedure

1. Point out how McCloskey uses the sense of hearing in his descriptive style:

    page 8 "Now you hear a million splashes."
    page 12 "Then through the fog you hear Harry Smith over at Blastow's Cove start the engine of his lobster boat and go out to pull his traps."
    page 14 "The forest is so quiet that you can hear an insect boring a tunnel deep inside a log."
    page 14 "And that other sound—is the sound of growing ferns, pushing aside dead leaves . . ."

2. Challenge students to think about the possibility of actually hearing ferns growing. Encourage discussion.
3. Have the students take the worksheets outside for the purpose of recording all the sounds—big and little—that they hear. Emphasize the importance of a quiet, no-talking atmosphere.
4. When students return, discuss their findings.

Taking It Further . . .

Repeat the activity, using one or more of the other five senses. Have the children go outside to record things they see, smell, or feel.

Name _____

The Sound of Growing Ferns and Other Things . . .

Directions: Shh! Listen. Record all the sounds you hear.

_____
_____
_____
_____
_____
_____
_____
_____
_____
_____
_____
_____
_____
_____
_____
_____

HISTORY

Materials:

•lined paper
•pencils

Lesson Procedure

1. Reread pages 54–57 in the book. Discuss the excitement of exploring, walking where no one has ever walked before, and discovering buried treasures from the past. The children in the story discovered an Indian shell heap under an old fallen tree.
2. Discuss archaeology and how archaeologists learn about past civilizations by exploring and digging.
3. Discuss who may have lived in your community fifty years ago, one hundred years ago, or hundreds of years ago.
4. Individually or in small groups, students can do research to find facts about former inhabitants of the area. Information can be found by interviewing local residents as well as through studying reference books.
5. After students have had time to gather data and share it with the class, have them make a mural showing the past and present cultures of their community.

Taking It Further . . .

Have students imagine that one hundred years from now an archaeologist will be digging up the ruins of their bedrooms. What would an archaeologist be able to tell about them based on the "treasures" found?

Time of Wonder

Henry

Henry Reed returns home from Europe to spend a summer with an aunt and uncle in New Jersey. He keeps a journal of his business ventures, adventures, and misadventures. An ordinary summer turns extraordinary, and Henry has a new understanding of what it is to be an American.

Additional Reading:
Henry Reed's Baby-sitting
Service, 1966
Henry Reed's Big Show, 1970
Henry Reed's Journey, 1963

Written by Keith Robertson
New York: Viking Press, 1958

Reed, Inc.

WRITING CLASSIFIED ADS

Materials:

- newspaper classified section
- lined paper
- pencils

Lesson Procedure

1. After reading "Sunday Night, June 23rd," have students write lost and found ads (real or imaginary).
2. Invite students to peruse the classified section of the newspaper for ideas. Explain that the charge for the ad is figured by the cost per line. Words need to be exact and not wasted.
3. Have students write several ads and then read the one they consider to be their best to the class.
4. Have students calculate the cost of their ads at $1.00 per line or $.25 per word.

Taking It Further . . .

For more practice writing classified ads, have students choose something that is visible in the room and write a descriptive ad for it. Have each child read his or her ad aloud while other class members try to guess what the ad describes.

> Found: Orange sphere.
> Bounces well, fits through a basketball hoop.
> Popular at recess.

Materials:

• lined paper
• pencils

Lesson Procedure

1. After reading "Monday, June 24th," have students discuss job possibilities for a boy or girl about ten years old. Ask students to tell about any jobs they may have had (baby-sitting, mowing the lawn, paper route).
2. Have students name jobs and occupations they would like to have when they get older. List them on the board. Then, go down the list and discuss the kinds of education or background a person would need to be successful in those positions.
3. Students can write short essays on the jobs they would like to have some day. Have students include why that job interests them, how they will achieve that position, and the salary they would like to receive.

Taking It Further . . .

Create job application forms for students applying for class-room jobs. Assign imaginary salaries for each job (play money or points).

✦ PROBLEM SOLVING ✦

Materials:

•lined paper
•pencils

Lesson Procedure

1. After reading "Thursday, July 4th," discuss the problem of locking the keys in your car and not being able to get in. Ask students to think of some possible solutions (calling the police, calling a friend to whom you have given a spare key, trying to "break in" your own car).
2. Discuss different ways people react to problems:

   Anger—threaten to sue or blame
   Frustration—now what?
   Facilitation—think of solutions

3. Encourage students to discuss how they usually react to problems and to give specific examples.

Taking It Further . . .

Warn the students that they will come to class the next day and face a problem. After they have gone, create a problem (mix up the desks, hide the textbooks, or remove the stapler). The next day have students discuss ways to deal with the problem and to solve it. After the problem is solved, discuss the students' feelings.

Henry Reed, Inc. ("Thursday, July 4th")

Materials:

- •worksheet on page 82
- •crayons or markers

Lesson Procedure

1. After reading "Wednesday, July 24th," have students decorate turtle shells, using the worksheet and crayons or markers.
2. Discuss symmetry and color.
3. Limit students to three colors to help them concentrate on balance in design.

Taking It Further . . .

Have students create original turtle shells, using upside-down egg cartons, clay, boxes, or origami.

Name _____

Directions: Decorate your turtle shell to achieve a balance of color and design.

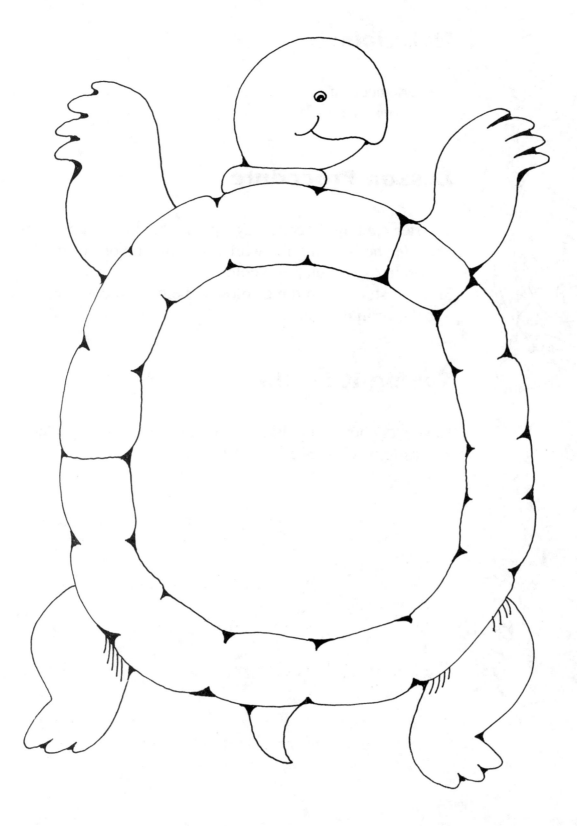

Henry Reed, Inc. ("Wednesday, July 24th")

The Robert McCloskey Connection © 1990 Fearon Teacher Aids

ALPHABETIZING

Materials:

- envelopes
- pencils

Lesson Procedure

1. After reading "Monday, July 29th," write a list of characters from the book on the chalkboard. Have students put the names in alphabetical order by the last name.

   Mr. Ainsworth
   Mr. Apple
   Mildred Doyle
   Midge Glass
   Al Harris
   Mr. Marble
   Mr. Mason
   Miss Prescott
   Henry Reed
   Mr. Sylvester

2. Divide the class into groups of four to six. Give each group enough envelopes to copy the names from the board.
3. Have each group shuffle the envelopes and trade them with another group. On a signal, each group sorts its envelopes alphabetically.

Taking It Further . . .

Assign zip codes to each envelope. Have the students sort the envelopes in numerical order from the lowest to highest number. This is an excellent way to review place value.

Materials:

Lesson Procedure

1. After reading "Thursday, August 1st," discuss the issue of man versus animals, wildlife control, and the balance of nature. Nature is kept in balance by the death of some animals and the birth of new ones. If either process is unnaturally disrupted, nature can become out of balance. Too many animals in a certain area can cause problems, such as an insufficient food supply to feed them all. Too few of a certain species can, of course, lead to extinction. Man hunting animals can cause nature to become out of balance, and so hunting seasons and other rules have been established.
2. Ask children if they can think of some justifiable reasons why animals should be hunted and killed (protection from harm by them, food use).
3. Many ranchers protect their herds of sheep by killing intruders such as wolves. Is that justifiable? What about the wolves? Will it create an imbalance in nature? Divide the class in half and have them debate the issue.

Taking It Further . . .

Students can create slogans or design posters to illustrate their views.

CREATIVE WRITING

Materials:

• worksheet on page 86
• pencils

Lesson Procedure

1. After reading "Thursday, August 22nd," discuss how Agony must have felt while on the balloon ride.
2. Hand out the worksheet and have students write a journal page entry from Agony's point of view. ("The first thing I noticed was that I was in a small basket with a cat. Then the basket seemed to be moving.")

Taking It Further . . .

After completing the book, encourage students to keep a personal journal of their own for a week or two.

Journal Entry

August 22

_____
_____
_____
_____
_____
_____
_____
_____
_____

agony

Henry Reed, Inc. ("Thursday, August 22nd")

Homer

The America that Norman Rockwell painted on canvas is captured by Robert McCloskey in the pages of *Homer Price*. Homer lives about two miles outside of Centerburg, where nothing happens, until Homer gets involved with robbers, an out-of-control doughnut machine, and an eccentric stranger.

Additional Reading:
Centerburg Tales, 1951

New York: Viking Press, 1943

Price

BEGINNING BLENDS

Materials:

- lined paper
- pencils

Lesson Procedure

1. After reading Chapter 1, discuss spoonerisms. A spoonerism is the transposition of initial sounds in two or more words. The sheriff says a spoonerism in the last line of the chapter, "That was sure one smell job of swelling, I mean one swell job of smelling!"

2. Have students try to figure out these spoonerisms:

   The twailer stopped trice. (The trailer stopped twice.)
   The tushy-bailed squirrels sampered scilently. (The bushy-tailed
   squirrels scampered silently.)
   Don't stray in the pleet. (Don't play in the street.)

3. Write a familiar nursery rhyme or quotation on the board, using spoonerisms. Have the students rewrite the passage correctly.

   Mittle liss Muffet tat on her suffet
   Eating her whurds and cey.
   Along spame a cider and sat bown deside her
   And mightened friss Muffet away.

4. Have students make up their own spoonerisms. Remind the students that if a word begins with a consonant blend, they need to exchange the entire blend with another letter or blend (smell, street/strell, smeet).

Taking It Further . . .

Have children listen for more of the sheriff's amusing spoonerisms as the story continues.

Homer Price (Chapter 1)

CREATIVE WRITING

Materials:

•unlined paper
•pencils

Lesson Procedure

1. After reading Chapter 2, discuss what makes a super-hero adventure (super attributes, a super challenge, and a super solution).
2. Make a list of super attributes on the board (read minds, arms as strong as steel, jump as high as a forty-story building).
3. Make a list of super challenges (stop a speeding train, travel across the country in ten minutes).
4. Have students write a new super-hero episode by combining a super challenge with some super attribute and coming up with a super solution.

Taking It Further . . .

Have students illustrate their episodes and combine them in a class book of "Super Stories."

❦ · VERBS · ❦

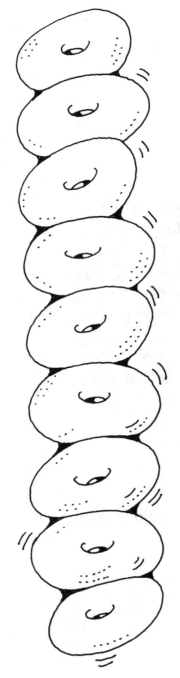

Materials:

•worksheet on page 91
•pencils

Lesson Procedure

1. After reading Chapter 3, discuss alternate ways to get rid of an abundance of doughnuts. Begin a list on the board of verbs that would solve the doughnut problem (eat, sell, burn, wear).
2. Have students continue making the list by writing a verb on each doughnut on the worksheet.

Taking It Further . . .

Make a batch of doughnuts with the class, using the following recipe.

Refrigerator-style baking powder biscuits
Cooking oil
Powdered sugar, cinnamon, or chocolate

Mold each biscuit into a doughnut shape by cutting a small hole in the center. Drop the molded biscuits into the hot oil, and fry until golden and puffy. Roll the doughnut in powdered sugar, cinnamon, or spread melted chocolate over the top and eat!

Too Many Doughnuts!

Directions: Think of as many verbs as you can that tell how to get rid of an abundance of doughnuts. Write one on each doughnut.

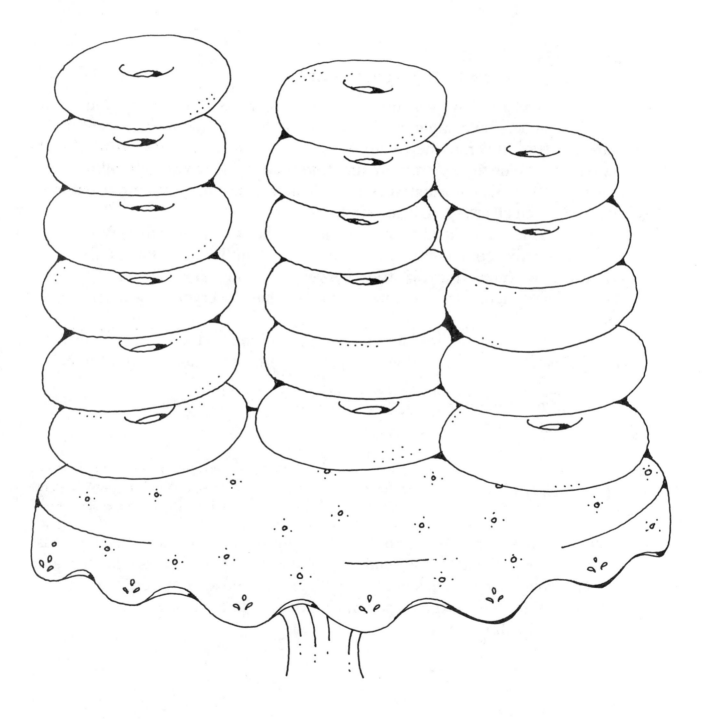

INTERDEPENDENCE

Materials:

•large ball of string or yarn

Lesson Procedure

1. After reading Chapter 4, have the students stand in a circle. Hand one student a ball of string. That student holds tightly onto the end of the string and then tosses the ball to another student across the circle.
2. The next student holds tightly onto the string and tosses the remaining ball across the circle to another student. Continue until all students are holding onto the string and a web has been created across the circle.
3. Discuss how we are interrelated to one another and must work together. When we work as a cooperative community, we are able to accomplish great things. On the count of three, everyone raises the string above their heads. The students will enjoy looking up at the pattern. Count to three again, and have everyone lower the string to the floor.
4. Toss the ball back, retracing the path of the string, rolling up the string with each toss. This takes time. Another option is to have one or two volunteers roll up the string.
5. With younger children, this activity works best if they sit on the floor and roll the string ball to each other.

Taking It Further . . .

Have the students make string balls. Students blow up small balloons and tie the ends. Provide small bowls of liquid starch. Students dip pieces of string or yarn in the starch and wrap them around the balloons until the balloons are mostly covered. Let the balloons dry overnight. The next day, pop the balloons with a pin and remove the pieces. A string ball will remain.

Homer Price (Chapter 4)

❧ • CREATIVE WRITING • ❧

Materials:

• worksheet on page 94
• pencils

Lesson Procedure

1. After reading Chapter 5, discuss other possible inventions that students could design (automatic dog feeder, homework machine, room cleaner-upper).
2. Have the students draw their inventions in the space provided on the worksheet and label the parts. Students can give their machines names, tell what they do, and how they work.

Taking It Further . . .

Encourage students to make 3-D models of their inventions at home and bring them in to show the class upon completion.

Name _____

My Invention

Draw your invention and label the parts.

[drawing box]

What is the name of your invention? _____

_____

What does your invention do? _____

_____

Describe how your invention works.

_____

_____

_____

_____

_____

The Robert McCloskey Connection © 1990 Fearon Teacher Aids

Materials:

• drawing paper

Lesson Procedure

1. After reading Chapter 6, teach all the children how to make the exact same type of paper airplane.

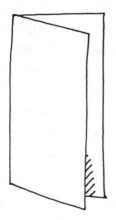

a. Fold paper in half lengthwise.

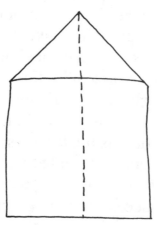

b. Open the paper and fold the corners of one end into the center, creating a point.

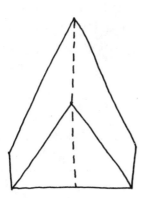

c. Fold corners in again, creating a sharper point.

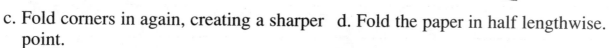

d. Fold the paper in half lengthwise.

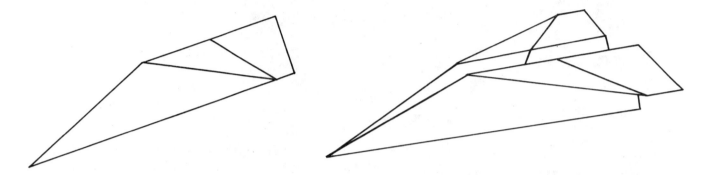

e. Fold the wings in half on each side.

2. Divide the class into two groups. Give both groups a stack of paper.
3. Instruct one group to make the airplanes, using an assembly line method. Each person on the line does one job and passes the airplane to the next line member. Have as many assembly lines as necessary to use every member of the group. Have the other half of the class make individual airplanes. Set a time limit. Instruct both groups to make as many airplanes as possible, according to the instructions.
4. When the time is up, have a spokesperson from each group report on the number of paper airplanes assembled within the time limit. Discuss the results and advantages or disadvantages of each method.
5. It may be necessary to have an inspection and disqualify any "inferior products."

Taking It Further . . .

Have a flight contest. Students enter their best paper airplanes in two or three categories (highest flight, longest air time, longest flight, trickiest flight, best-looking aircraft, or funniest aircraft). No prizes are necessary. The students enjoy the show.